I0794330

THIS BOOK

Written and compiled by Deborah Lock
Illustrations copyright © 2008 Tina Macnaughton
This edition copyright © 2022 Lion Hudson IP Limited

All unattributed prayers are by Deborah Lock, Sophie Piper and Lois Rock, copyright © 2008, 2022 Lion Hudson IP Limited

All rights reserved. No part of this publication may be reproduced or transmitted in any form or by any means, electronic or mechanical, including photocopy, recording, or any information storage and retrieval system, without permission in writing from the publisher.

Published by **Lion Children's Books**
www.lionhudson.com
Part of the SPCK Group
SPCK, 36 Causton Street, London, SW1P 4ST

ISBN 978 0 7459 7937 3

Some materials in this book first published in
An Arkful of Animal Prayers © 2008

This edition © 2022

Acknowledgments
Prayers on pp. 54, 56, 57 and 58 based on Psalms 23, 65 and 96 from the Good News Bible Translation, © 1994 published by the Bible Societies/ HarperCollins Publishers Ltd UK, Good News Bible © American Bible Society 1966, 1971, 1976, 1992. Used with permission. Also the International Children's Bible ® Copyright © 1986, 1988, 1999, 2015 by Tommy Nelson™, a division of Thomas Nelson. Used by permission.

A catalogue record for this book is available from the British Library

Printed and bound in China, October 2021, LH54

PRAYERS FOR WILD ANIMALS

THEIR HABITATS AND THE ENVIRONMENT

ILLUSTRATED BY TINA MACNAUGHTON

LION CHILDREN'S

"Noah," said God, "build me a boat
that's long and wide and sure to float.
Then search the whole world through and through,
and fetch the creatures, two by two.

"Bring them from their quiet green places
and their lairs in wild, wide spaces.
Call the birds down from the air.
All the beasts are now in your care.

"Keep them quite safe from flood and rain
till all the world is clean again.
Olives grow, a sign from the dove,
and rainbows bend down from above."

CONTENTS

QUIET GREEN PLACES

The little bugs that scurry,
the little beasts that creep
among the grasses and the weeds
and where the leaves are deep:
all of them were made by God
as part of God's design.
Remember that the world is theirs,
not only yours and mine.

Bless our little garden.
May it be a safe place for all the little creatures
that creep and scurry through the grasses.
May it be a busy place for the little creatures
that sip and nibble and munch
among the flowers.
May it be a joyful place for all the birds
that sing and nest in the trees.

Thank you for the rabbits
that hop and run around
as they nibble at the grass.
Bless their homes underground.

Creator God,
The cycle of life is a wonder to see.
Out of a simple egg wriggles a caterpillar
that crawls from leaf to leaf
and eats and eats and eats.

Until one day, it spins a cocoon
to rest and hide away,
transforming into a completely new life –
a brilliant butterfly, fluttering in the light.

O God,
Let me stop and see
the tiny creatures that are around me:
the dancing butterflies fluttering
from flower to flower,
the busy bees gathering nectar hour by hour,
the ants, the beetles, and the bugs,
and slithering ones like worms and slugs.
Keep them safe in your care and
bless them all, everywhere.

All things bright and beautiful,
all creatures great and small,
all things wise and wonderful,
the Lord God made them all.

Cecil Frances Alexander (1818–95)

God of rabbits,
God of toads,
help all creatures
cross the roads.

In their burrows and in their nests,
keep your creatures safe as they rest.
Keep them warm and keep them dry,
protect them from any danger nearby.

Dear God,
The work of your creatures,
like the marching ants,
keeps the Earth in perfect balance.
Each has a place and a role to play.
May we respect and admire
all that they do as they work together
for they are loved and known by you.

Bless the ever-busy spider, spinning a web
that glimmers in the morning dew,
as a net to catch its prey
so that it can live another day.

WiLD WiDE SPACES

I think of the great variety
of all the creatures on earth:
the great and powerful,
the small and timid.
I think of their secrets
and curious ways
and my heart longs
to sing their Creator's praise.

Dear God,
I wonder at all the eye-catching
patterns in nature:
the spots, the stripes, the patches, and the bold.
They help the hunters and the hunted
to blend into their surroundings,
to warn their family of danger,
to warn other creatures they don't taste good
and to help them impress to find a mate.

Help us, dear God,
to learn from all wild animals:
how to live in harmony
with our land,
how to live in peace
with those who are unlike us,
how to enjoy the beauty of life,
and how to accept death.

From the plains of the savanna
to the hot dry deserts,
may these lands be respected
and the animals protected
from human actions and destruction.

May herds graze in safety and
the trees and grasses flourish.
May there be a plentiful supply
of food and water.
May the young be wild and free.

O God,
Love the creatures that are not loved
and those that are greatly feared.
The scavengers that take the scraps,
the dung beetles that process the waste,
the biters and the stingers
that protect themselves and their homes.
Let me remember that you created them
and care for them.

All things bright and beautiful,
all creatures great and small,
all weevils, worms, and warthogs,
the Lord God made them all.

Thank you, God,
for yawning hippos, keeping cool
in the muddy pools.

Thank you, God,
for cheeky monkeys, swinging
from branch to branch.

Thank you, God,
for stomping elephants, flapping ears
and swinging trunks.

Thank you, God,
for…

In the heat of the sun,
may animals find shade
to lie down and rest.
Protect them from those
who want to harm them.

O God,
May there be an end to poaching
so animals can live in peace.

O God,
When land gets dry and parched,
I think of the animals holding on.

When fires break out, may help be near.
May their lives be free from fear.

Dear God,
Where the glaciers are melting
and the sea ice drifts apart.
Where the waves are rising
and the land is washed away.
When times are tough,
and food is hard to find.
Give strength to the animals
whose lands are changing.

I listen to the sounds of the animals
that are out and about at night.
The howls and the hoots,
the screeches and the snuffles.
God, hear their cries and answer their calls.

Curled-up animals, O God, safely keep
snug and warm through their long winter's sleep.

For all creatures of the oceans,
may we keep the waters clear and blue.
God, help us be of help to them,
so that they can enjoy life, too.

Let us keep the beaches clean,
Let not all the fish be caught,
Let us protect the coral reefs,
Keep oceans safe for every sort.

LOOK TO THE SKIES

The sound of birdsong
in the morning air
reminds me that heaven's music
reaches everywhere.

The kingdom of God
is like a tree
growing through all eternity.
In its branches, birds may nest;
in its shade we all may rest.

Hungry chicks, busy birds,
Our Father, feeds them –
so much more will He feed us.

O God,
When the wintry season draws near,
many birds prepare to fly.
Guide their flight,
make safe their way,
until their journey ends.

May my spirit soar like a bird,
wheeling and dipping through the sky
with the joy of knowing you.

When new shoots spring up,
God bless the birds twittering in the trees,
fluttering in the hedgerows,
and soaring upon the breeze.

When days are long and warm,
God bless the birds gathering on the shore,
gliding above the ocean
where breakers crash and roar.

When leaves start to fall,
God bless the birds preparing to fly,
filling the damp and chilly air
with wild and eager cry.

When days are dark and cold,
God bless the birds hopping across the snow,
pecking the fallen seeds and fruits
of summer long ago.

HOPE FOR OUR WORLD

Our world is the Lord's
and God gave its care to us.

Let us be resourceful,
let us be respectful,
let us be responsible.

Let us always remember:
hope for the animals
lies in our care.

Lord of the ocean,
Lord of the sea:
let all the fish swim
strong and free.

Lord of the waves,
Lord of the shore:
keep them all safe
for evermore.

I plant a tree for the earth.
I plant a tree for the air.
I plant a tree for the whole wide world
that God gave us all to share.

Help us to care for creatures all
be they large or be they small,
so we can all enjoy your creation
and rejoice in God in every nation.

Reduce, reuse, recycle.
What do we need and use?
Reduce our waste, our water, and fuel
to be good news to the Earth.

Reduce, reuse, recycle.
How does our world stay clean?
Repair and share, recycle, make new
and keep our whole Earth green.

Dear God, you are our shepherd,
you give us all we need,
you lead to where the grass grows green
and animals can safely feed.

You take them where the water
is quiet and cool and clear;
and there they rest and know they're safe
for you are always near.

From Psalm 23 [based on GNB]

O God,
The whole world stands in wonder
of the great things that you have done.
You care for the land by sending rain;
you make the soil rich and fertile.
You fill the streams with water;
you provide the earth with crops.

From Psalm 65 [based on GNB]

Sing to the Lord, all the world!
Be glad, earth and sky!
Roar, sea, and every creature in you;
rejoice, fields, and every animal in you!
Then all the trees in the forest will sing for joy.

From Psalm 96 [based on GNB/ICB]

God of Noah,
who sent the flood:
help us to clean the earth of all that pollutes it.

God of Noah,
who sent the rainbow:
restore the pattern of the seasons,
that there may be summer and winter
and seedtime and harvest.

God of Noah:
keep us safe in the ark of your love.
May we have faith to keep us from sinking,
hope for a better tomorrow,
and love for all that you have made.

Inspired by Genesis 7–8

My Prayer for Wild Animals

INDEX OF FIRST LINES